THE STATE & THE SLUMS.

By EDWARD STANLEY ROBERTSON.

Published at the Central Offices of the
LIBERTY AND PROPERTY DEFENCE LEAGUE,
4, WESTMINSTER CHAMBERS, LONDON, S.W.

1884.

In the interest of creating a more extensive selection of rare historical book reprints, we have chosen to reproduce this title even though it may possibly have occasional imperfections such as missing and blurred pages, missing text, poor pictures, markings, dark backgrounds and other reproduction issues beyond our control. Because this work is culturally important, we have made it available as a part of our commitment to protecting, preserving and promoting the world's literature. Thank you for your understanding.

NOTE.—Part of this essay was written before Mr. Chamberlain's paper in the *Fortnightly Review* appeared, and the comments on that paper in the concluding pages were in MS. before the third week of December, 1883.

THE STATE AND THE SLUMS.

MANY well-meaning persons, and some by no means stupid ones, would declare that it is not State-socialism at all, to devise schemes for the better housing of the poor at the cost of imperial or municipal funds. This, however, is not the opinion of Socialists themselves. They are not, indeed, prepared to give a release in full of all demands, in return for a measure such as is now under discussion; but they distinctly intimate that they would consider such a measure an instalment of their full claim, and an acknowledgment of its substantial justice. Mr. H. M. Hyndman, the chairman of the Democratic Federation, thus expresses himself in the *Pall Mall Gazette* of October 29, 1883: "The workers being able to get better rooms at lower rents could afford to take lower wages in time of pressure, and consequently so much would be deducted from their competition wages when next they came forward to struggle with one another for employment." And he goes on—"*There it is;* look at it how you will, *there is the curse of our present system.* Competition for gain above; competition for *bare subsistence wages below*" These words go to the root of the whole matter, as doubtless they were intended to do. Unless society is reconstructed on the basis of which Mr. Hyndman and his friends approve, they treat such remedies as are offered by way of palliative, as a mere admission of the extreme principle for which they are contending. Nevertheless, Mr. Hyndman's words contain an important truth. The question is at bottom a question of wages. As he says, give men better lodgings for the same or less rent, and they will be tempted to accept lower wages when competition comes on them; but even this is not all. Some of them will be tempted to add to their actual wages by sub-letting; with what consequences, in one way or another, we shall see presently. In the meantime it might be well to look at the matter from another point of view. On the very same day (29th October, 1883) on which the *Pall Mall Gazette* published Mr. Hyndman's paper, there appeared a letter in the *St. James's Gazette* purporting to be from a real workingman. This writer says, "the press and the very respectables seem to be making a particular row at present about that one of our troubles that happens to offend their eyes the most and perhaps affect their precious health." And he goes on to point out that from the point of view of the genuine working-man, overcrowding is not such a very great nuisance as it is alleged by the philanthropists to be. There is a good deal more in the letter which would well repay perusal, but its special merit is that it conveys a caution to those reformers who insist upon amending the poor man's lot without taking the poor man himself into council. Overcrowding, beyond any doubt, is a bad thing; it is the fertile source both of disease and of vice. But it is not always what the amateur philanthropist would call overcrowding which the poor themselves feel to be such. Overcrowding often simply means warmth. A thinly inhabited and highly ventilated room is apt to be a cold room, and underfed people are sensitive to cold. Those who are underfed are apt also to be ill-clad, and are pretty certain not to have the means of purchasing much fuel. Hence, independently of the low rents of crowded lodgings, the mere warmth of them is a temptation to the very poor. Thus we have two causes which make it a doubtful boon for the poor to be offered cheap, spacious, and well-ventilated dwellings. The cheapness would probably react on their wages; the space and the ventilation would only be a change in their discomfort. Foul air and evil smells they are used to; cold, kept away by the very things that bring the foul air and the smells, they escape in their homes. They have enough and to spare of it out of doors, and naturally they do not care to be pursued by it farther than they must.

And even when all this has been said, the subject is very far from being exhausted. Indeed, the most serious difficulty of all remains behind. Clean, spacious, and well-ventilated lodgings may be provided; but how are they to be kept clean and well ventilated, and how are the occupants to be prevented from overcrowding them in the future? Let the difficulty about wages be waived for argument's sake—though, if Mr. Hyndman is right, it will arise the very moment competition sets in—yet there will remain the cold of the new lodgings, which will be a permanent temptation. The first effort to contend with this will probably take the shape of stopping up ventilators, unless, indeed, these are so cunningly hidden that the occupants of the house cannot get at them. But it will not be very long before people begin to find out that a dozen persons in a room twelve feet square are much more "snug" than three or four, and that the kind of coarse comfort which comes from mere heat is not inconsistent with almost any amount of what fine ladies and gentlemen call "stuffiness." How are people to be hindered from working their will in this way? In many cases the mere increase of families will overcrowd the lodging, without any intrusion from outside. A man and his wife can do well enough in one decent room, and are actually comfortable in two; but when there are five children what is to be done? Be it remembered that in the rank of life we are dealing with, wages do not increase to any great extent after marriage, and certainly not in the same ratio as families increase. Indeed, it might be said, without much inaccuracy, that a working-man would be in receipt of his highest wages about the time of his marriage, or very soon after it. The family resources would not begin to increase until the children in their turn began to earn wages, and that time is now almost fixed by law at a minimum age of thirteen years. In fourteen years an average couple would almost certainly have five children, and might have seven or more. Before the eldest child, therefore, could contribute anything to the family resources, there would probably be seven human beings, and might easily be nine, ten or even twelve, to occupy the space originally calculated for two. How is this state of things to be prevented or remedied? I showed in a former paper *(Communism)* that in order to equalise wages and keep them fixed, it would be necessary to invest the State-appointed captains of industry with some power of checking the increase of families. But this brings the thing still nearer home. It now appears that this kind of power—a power, the very mention of which seems to require an apology, so abhorrent is it to our feelings as Englishmen—this power, I say, would have to be exercised in order to keep the lodgings of the working-class in the condition wherein the philanthropist would have them. This one cause alone would in time baffle the most rigorous system of regulation, inspection, and supervision. But would any supervision be sufficient to check sub-letting? It would no doubt be possible to start a certain number of new tenement houses which should be under very stringent regulation. Already there are model lodging-houses, Peabody mansions, Miss Octavia Hill's improved courts. These things are a success, and all honour to those who have made them so. But the managers of these institutions would themselves readily admit that their success is at least partly due to the fact that the incorrigibles— the people who would be bound by no rules, and submit to no supervision—all went away and pigged in uninspected rookeries. The rookery is a very horrible thing, but it is a safety valve. There is no alternative. Either you must inspect and regulate every house where any poor people can by any possibility lodge, or you must tolerate the rookery in the long run. The evil may be, and ought to be, reduced to the very lowest expression; but it can no more be got rid of than the incorrigibles and ne'er-do-wells of any class of society can be got rid of in a general massacre. The late Mr. Thomas Carlyle talked a great deal of hysterical nonsense about the gallows and grapeshot for those whom he called "devil's regiments." Our socialistic philanthropists of to-day are always formulating projects whose ultimate sanction would need to be something of the Carlylese gallows or grape—a sanction they would never dream of applying in hard fact. Once more, then, we find ourselves face to face with the old dilemma. So long as the shiftless and flabby-minded folk are there, socialism, piecemeal or wholesale, is impracticable. Once they are got rid of it is no longer wanted. If piecemeal Socialism is to be put in practice, it will not be long before it becomes wholesale Socialism. But as a matter of fact it will never be put in practice. We shall probably see the building of a good many new model lodgings, some by private beneficence and some, perhaps, with public money. A certain number of "slums" and "rookeries" will be pulled down, and their inhabitants will again herd where they can, so that not impossibly their last state will be worse than their first. I am not defending the rookery, but simply pointing out the great difficulties that lie in the way of its reform or abolition. The most carefully constructed lodging may become a rookery in the course of time, by the mere multiplication of the family inhabiting it. This is an evil which no inspection or manipulation will cure. But unless every house were placed under inspection where any working people might under any circumstances lodge, the process of creating rookeries would be a much more rapid one. Every one who disliked inspection—and their name is legion—would abandon the inspected houses. The evil in short lies deeper than can be reached either by Mr. Hyndman's revolutionary remedy of a State regulation of wages, or the popular remedy of a State inspection of houses. *Apropos* of this question of inspection, it is edifying to observe how the journals that discuss the housing of the poor, from the *Pall Mall* on the left to *St. James's* on the right, one and all manifest distrust of the elected bodies—the vestries—in whose hands at present rests the enforcing of sanitary laws. One correspondent contrasts the good effect of police inspection under the Common Lodging-Houses Act with the carelessness or selfishness of vestrymen and vestry doctors in regard to the sanitation of tenement houses. Another insinuates, or rather, openly declares, that vestrymen are themselves causes of the grievance. So many of them are owners of tenement houses, that they cannot (he says) be trusted to abate nuisances when the cost will come directly or indirectly out of their own pockets. I am not concerned to defend negligence or selfishness, where it is shown to exist; but I refer to what has been said above as suggesting that in a very large number of cases the obstruction to improvement and sanitation is quite as much the work of the lodgers as of the lodging-house keepers, to say nothing of the actual house owner. As regards these last, indeed, there seems to be no pleasing the philantrophist and the eager politician. Now it is the Duke of . . . . who is being denounced as a harsh and cruel head landlord, because his agent takes somewhat abrupt measures for pulling down a tenement house whose middleman lessee has absconded, and which is becoming a nuisance through the neglect or misconduct of the lodgers. Anon it is all the fault of the middleman lessee, who is painted in the blackest of colours as a bloated, grasping, selfish capitalist, wringing sixty or seventy per cent out of the sweat and tears of the poor. As a matter of fact the lessee is quite often enough one of the poor himself—or herself, for tenement houses in a very appreciable number of instances belong to women. As regards the sixty or seventy per cent, some part must certainly be set down to repairs and maintenance of the fabric of the house. A good deal may be fairly written off against the risk and trouble of collection. When all allowances are made, one may be permitted to doubt whether much more is really to be accounted profit than would be held to deserve that name in the case of other trades. However that may be, it would seem as if we were entering upon an era of new and very questionable morality in this matter of the relation of landlord and tenant. Already in one part of the kingdom the rules of contract, and the principles of political economy have been banished to Jupiter and Saturn. In the very heart of the kingdom attempts have been made to apply the same methods to the same subject-matter. The letting and hiring of agricultural land is now in a great measure taken out of the domain of free contract, and legislation is manifesting a tendency to abolish contract wholly where land is concerned. We are now threatened with an application of the same process to houses. It is openly asserted that houseowners make too much out of their property; and it is but a short step from this to asserting that their profits ought to be cut down by a tribunal. Nor is this all. So very tender are we becoming of what we suppose to be the comfort of the poor, that we seem to be on the point of depriving them of the greatest comfort of all—personal freedom. How many members of the middle class would endure for a week the inspection and " ordering about" which our philanthropic reformers are never tired of inflicting on their poorer neighbours? And is it not clear that even a greater amount of inspection and " ordering about" would have to be resorted to, if the homes of the people are to be kept in the condition in which the reformers would have them? Is it not true that the respectable, clean, well-to-do working-men and women (of whom there are hundreds of thousands in London, and millions throughout the kingdom) would have to be harassed day and night in order that the inspector and the philanthropist might get at the dirty, disreputable, idle, pauperised vagabond, three parts loafer and the rest thief? As to the real thieves, burglars, and their congeners—it is at least allowable to doubt whether the inspector and the philanthropist would ever sweep them into the net at all. Whether they did or not, certain it is that the capture could only be attempted—not to say accomplished—by placing the entire working community under a *regime* practically undistinguishable from slavery. The question is therefore a working-man's question in the very fullest sense of the words. It may be possible for the rich to offer the present generation of the poor the most munificent gifts in the way of new and improved dwellings. But will the poor be able to keep them? Will not the gift react upon wages, as Mr. Hyndman suggests? Will not something be given with one hand and taken with the other? Do people really like model dwellings?

Will not the natural increase of the family fill up the model dwelling, not, indeed, as fast as subletting would, but faster than wages will keep pace with? Will not subletting itself be a chronic temptation, needing a slave driver in the uniform of an inspector to keep it away from the door? These are questions that rich men should ask themselves before they formulate crude schemes of law-enforced philanthrophy; they are questions, above all, that the poor should ask the rich, before they welcome such schemes.

One word of caution. I am not attacking philanthropy, nor even suggesting that our social arrangements in this and other matters are open to no improvement. I am not even deprecating State interference, except in so far as I find myself forced to conclude that State interference would be either nugatory or mischievous. There is still plenty of room for State activity, in the prevention and punishment of crime, for instance, without trenching upon the personal freedom of citizens who are not criminals. Nay, even in this very matter of the sanitation of poor people's dwellings (for it is mainly a question of sanitation in the long run) there is plenty of room for State activity in providing cheaper and more accessible procedure for the abatement of nuisances, to be put in motion by the people whom the nuisances annoy, and not by a staff of paid officials. Enough has not been done in this direction; when all has been done that can be done, then, and not till then, it will be time to think of starting an official agency. And lastly be it said that all which has been written above applies to State philanthropy. For private effort we have no criticism but praise, and no sentiment but good-will.

So much for the main subject. But something requires to be said, I think, about Mr. Chamberlain's article in the *Fortnightly Review*. I leave it to the daily papers, and to those who deal with the matter from the point of view of party politics, to comment upon this attempt of the Radical Codlin to outbid the Conservative Short. But it is worth while pointing out to those interested in the defence of liberty and property, that Mr. Chamberlain writes quite as much in the capacity of a party man, as in that of a social reformer. Here are the concluding words of his article.

"It remains to be seen whether practical effect can at present be given to the only measures which afford hope of permanent relief, or whether we shall be condemned to witness yet another tinkering of the machinery which has entirely broken down. In this case it will be our duty to point out to the people at large that what they want done they must secure for themselves. Political power is only the means to an end—the extension of the suffrage and redistribution of seats would indeed be as worthless as the vacation essays of great landowners if they did not lead directly to the practical solution of some of those social questions which intimately concern the welfare of the masses of the people, and in the settlement of which they have a just right to make their voices heard."

In these words the politician speaks, and not the social reformer. Mr. Chamberlain affects to want a particular improvement in social arrangements. We shall see presently that in attempting to bring about this alleged improvement, he proposes to make an attack on the rights of property generally, and especially on the rights of landed proprietors. He can see no other way to his purpose than to demand vast political changes, about the expediency of which public opinion is to a great extent in suspense. It would hardly be unfair to say that he is thinking of political projects first, and of social reforms only "a bad second." These, however, are considerations for party politicians. Our business is to see how his proposals affect liberty and property.

In the following passages will be found the key note of his whole essay.

"Whatever may be the truth as to the present position of the labourer [*i.e.*, agricultural], it is certain that the improvement, if there is any in his lot, is due to that destruction of dwellings and depopulation of the country which has been carried out on so many estates, and which has been constantly increasing the competition and overcrowding in the towns. This migration from the land is a constant phenomenon. It aggravates all the evils of town life, reduces wages, increases the pressure for accommodation, and accounts in part for the acuteness of the distress which prevails.

* * * * * *

It may be safely asserted that no satisfactory settlement of social questions will be reached until the arbitrary and anomalous system by which in England alone of all the great civilised countries the actual tillers of the soil are practically forbidden even the hope of ownership, has been changed into something more humane and sensible; but this is a remedy not dreamt of in Lord Salisbury's philosophy, and foreign to the immediate purpose of the present article."

Mr. Chamberlain fancies himself to have a mission to redress the English system of land tenure. We shall see presently that his practical remedy (so far as he has not borrowed it from some more moderate politicians) seems to have been framed under the influence of theories not unlike those of Mr. Henry George, the American agrarian socialist. Mr. Chamberlain may well say that his attack upon the tenure of agricultural land is foreign to the purpose of his essay. No one, reasoning calmly, could for a moment suppose that any amount of peasant proprietorship could diminish the crowding of towns *by certain classes*, and those the classes who do crowd towns, break or evade sanitary laws, and vex the souls of the inspector and the philanthropist. But let us turn to the remedies actually proposed by Mr. Chamberlain. These are given in seven formal paragraphs, which we extract. But they are prefaced by a statement of a very general and very remarkable nature, upon which it will be necessary to make some comment. The seven paragraphs, meantime, may be summed up in a very few words, with which neither politician, nor social reformer, nor social conservative, will be at all likely to disagree. "Make sanitary law stronger where it appears necessary to do so; and make it easier to work the sanitary laws that exist." This (omitting the preamble) is the entire sum and substance of the extracts that follow, and it is a very remarkable fact that a great many of Mr. Chamberlain's suggestions are law already.

The expense of making towns habitable for the toilers who dwell in them must be thrown on the land which their toil makes valuable, and without any effort on the part of its owners. When these owners, not satisfied with the unearned increment which the general prosperity of the country has created, obtain exorbitant returns from their investment by permitting arrangements which make their property a public nuisance and a public danger, the State is entitled to step in and deprive them of the rights which they have abused, paying only such compensation as will fairly represent the worth of their property fairly used.

1. The law should make it an offence, punishable by heavy fine, to own property in a state unfit for human habitation. The law already punishes the retail tradesman who exposes diseased meat for sale, and it is a much more serious offence to make a profit out of conditions which are absolutely incompatible with health and morality.

2. In every case in which the local authority acquires property under these conditions the arbitrator should be empowered to deduct from the ascertained value such sum as he thinks fit by way of fine for the misuse of the property and the offence committed in allowing it to be the cause of disease and crime.

3. Local authorities should have power, subject only to appeal to the High Court, to close such property, or to make at the expense of the owner such alterations or repairs as may be ordered by the sanitary officer, without being compelled to acquire it.

4. Local authorities should be further empowered to acquire any lands and buildings for the purpose of a scheme under the Artisans' Dwellings Acts, at the fair market value of the same, to be settled by an arbitrator appointed for the purpose, and instructed to give in every case *the value which a willing seller would obtain in the open market from a private purchaser, with no allowance for prospective value or compulsory sale.*

6. The scheme of improvement should include any surrounding property which will be benefited by the reconstruction of an unhealthy area, and the confirming order should authorise a rate to be levied on the owners of such adjacent property, fairly representing the appreciation of their holding by the proposed improvement. The principle of this proposal has always been adopted in the case of town improvements in the United States, and it has even found its way into English legislation. The Artisans' Dwellings Act, 1882, provides that when in the opinion of the arbitrator the demolition of the property dealt with adds to the value of other property belonging to the same owner, the amount of such increased value may be apportioned and levied as an improvement rate on the lands, &c., affected; and a similar provision has been inserted in a Provisional Order, 1879, obtained by the Corporation of Liverpool. All that is now required is to extend this principle to all lands benefited, whether belonging to the same owner or not.

7. The cost of any scheme for the reconstruction of an unhealthy area should be levied on all owners of property, including long leaseholders, within a certain district to be determined by the scheme. The promoters would, in fact, in every case specify a contributory district, and the official sent to conduct an inquiry into the scheme would decide whether or not it had been rightly defined. The contributory district might be, in London, the whole metropolis, or, in the provinces, the whole borough; but if the improvement were essentially local in its character and likely to be to the immediate advantage of a more limited district, the cost might be thrown entirely on the owners within such district.

When due allowance has been made for the somewhat violent language in which these suggestions are put forward, it will be seen that they do not differ in substance from those urged by Earl Grey, in a very wise and temperate letter to the *Times* of 24th November, 1883. Whether the remedies suggested by the Earl or the Capitalist would work, is a matter for practical consideration. For reasons given in former pages, I am myself tempted to think that neither set of suggestions could or would do all that is expected. But the remarkable part of Mr. Chamberlain's project of legislation is its preamble. Is it possible he can really think that the ground landlords in London, or in any other town, are responsible for the condition of the houses in which " toilers " dwell? If Mr. Chamberlain were not misled by a theoretical prejudice against landed property in general, he could not fail to see that the one thing a ground landlord cannot do is to obtain a profit out of " arrangements which make his property a public nuisance." A landlord leases his sites in the first instance to builders, for periods of great length. When the building leases fall in, and the houses become the landlord's direct property, it is almost invariably an object with him to lease them for periods, shorter indeed than the original building lease, but always of considerable length. As long as houses are in the hands of a building lessee, or his representatives, the ground landlord can derive no profit from them beyond the rent reserved in the lease, and can exercise no control over them outside the covenants contained in that document. Even when the buildings come into the landlord's own hands, he almost invariably proceeds to make fresh arrangements whereby the control passes from himself to some one who is more or less of a middleman between the head landlord and the occupant who lets lodgings or tenements. It is a very rare thing, indeed, to find a London house let by the year, or for less than three years, even to the person supposed to be the immediate occupant. Seven years is probably the commonest period of agreement in an occupancy letting. What is true of London is true, *mutatis mutandis*, of all large towns in England, Ireland, and Scotland. It may safely be asserted that in not one case in a thousand is the ground landlord also the tenement lessor. Consequently, it is entirely untrue to assert of ground landlords as a class, that they obtain exorbitant returns from their investment by permitting their property to become a public nuisance and a public danger. Mr. Chamberlain, indeed, tries to make out a case, by insinuating that ground landlords, when overcrowded and dilapidated buildings have been taken up under the Artisans' Dwellings Act, have charged heavy prices for the sites. We give his argument in a note, simply asking in reply, how much of the money he speaks of went into the pockets of ground landlords? how much into the pockets of their lessees? and how comes it that ground "sold with the obligation to build workmen's dwellings" is worth only 3s. 4d. per foot? If, as Mr. Chamberlain's authority states, the land in question was worth 10s. a foot "for commercial purposes," what right has he to take it for workmen's dwellings at 3s. 4d.? Until these questions are answered, Mr. Chamberlain's argument is worth very little. *

---

* The Report of the Committee of the House of Commons (June, 1882,) presided over by Sir Richard Cross, gives a full account of the operations in the metropolis under the Acts of 1875 and 1879. The Metropolitan Board of Works have dealt in all with forty-two acres of land, inhabited by 20,335 persons. The net loss on the improvement is estimated at £1,211,336, or about £60 per head of the population assumed to be benefited. The cost of the land required has been about 17s. per square foot. The price obtainable for the same land, if sold with the obligation to build workman's dwellings, is 3s. 4d. per foot on the average, but its value for commercial purposes is stated to be 10s. per foot. The inference from these figures is most important; but, strangely enough, the Committee do not seem to have drawn it. Under Sir R. Cross's Acts, which were "intended to guard against any excessive valuation of the property dealt with," it appears that the owners of houses, courts, and alleys which had been declared by the proper authority unfit for human habitation, receive 17s. per foot for land which could not be valued, even after the improvements had been made and new streets laid out, at more than 10s. per foot for commercial purposes, or more than 3s. 4d. per foot for artisans' dwellings. In other words, the effect of expropriation in the case of those owners, whose laches and criminal neglect had brought about the state of things which required State intervention, was that they made a profit of

The truth probably is that the cost of 17s. per square foot was made up of payment to the ground landlord, and compensation not only to the immediate lessor of the tenements, but to the holders of interests intervening between the ground freehold and the tenement owner. To these sums we should also have to add the cost of demolition, so that land whose *net* value, unbuilt on, might be only 10s. a foot, would easily come to 17s. before it was cleared. As to 3s. 4d. a foot " sold with the obligation to build workmen's dwellings," if the land is worth 10s. for commercial purposes, it would be sheer robbery to force a sale for 3s. 4d. because it happened to be wanted for workmen's lodgings. Land, like any other commodity, is worth as much as it will fetch in open market ; and if philanthropists or social Utopia-mongers want land in the heart of a great city, they must pay the market price for it, and not fix a low fancy price, any more than they would allow the owner to fix a high fancy price.

It seems, then, that we may safely assume the following propositions. First, ground landlords are not, and cannot be as a rule, directly responsible for the use made of house property. Secondly, they are indirectly responsible only in so far as the use made of such property contravenes covenants in the leases on which it is held. Thirdly, the compensation value in cases where demolition has to take place includes the cost of demolition, and compensation for all interests, primary, derivative, and ultimate. The first of these principles negatives Mr. Chamberlain's dogma

---

7s. per foot on the ordinary market value of their property under the most favourable circumstances, and that they obtained 13s. 8d. per foot more than their land was fairly worth for the special purpose for which they had been employing it. It is not surprising, under these circumstances, that the Committee report that " The difficulty in carrying out the provisions of these Acts obviously arises from the great cost of doing so." In fact, the Acts as at present worked offer a premium for neglect and wilful indifference to sanitary provisions. They say, in effect, to the bad landlord, " Allow your property to fall into disrepair, to become a nest of disease, and a centre of crime and immorality, and then we will step in and buy it from you at a price seventy per cent. above what you could obtain in the ordinary market if you attempted to dispose of it without our assistance."

that the cost of improvement must fall on the land exclusively. The second does, indeed, throw upon the ground landlords the duty (which we do not deny) of seeing that their leases are properly drawn, and that the covenants in them are observed. But would Mr. Chamberlain propose, for instance, to make it a universal covenant in every building lease that the building lessee shall not sublet? That could hardly stand. Is the building lessee then to be bound always to covenant with his sub-lessees not to sublet? If not, where is the line to be drawn? One correspondent of a daily paper has, indeed, suggested that ground landlords ought to be held responsible for seeing that the repairing covenants in their leases are properly observed, and that the houses are kept in good order throughout the tenancy, instead of being merely repaired at the expiring of a lease. This is very well as far as it goes; but it does not meet a great deal of the case, and it would be very hard to carry out. It does nothing to check overcrowding; and it does not touch a certain aspect of matters pointedly referred to by Mr. Chamberlain in the passage quoted below.* In these words we have another instance of the curious inability of the Socialist theorist to see the practical aspect of his

---

* "There is a certain class of property always found in these unhealthy areas and used for immoral purposes actually prohibited by the law. The illegal occupation is, however, the justification of the exorbitant rents demanded from the wretched occupants by the persons who trade in their vices. A house which for honest occupation is worth £50 a year will bring in double or treble to an owner who winks at the traffic which it is permitted to shelter. When this house is required by the local authority, the demand for compensation is based, and often allowed, on an income which represents not a fair return for an investment but the profit on complicity with vice. The same result obtains where tenements which could properly accommodate a single family are made to do duty for three or four times as many persons as can be decently housed in them. The income derived is proportionately increased, and compensation follows as a premium on evil practices. Accordingly men are found to speculate on the probability of interference, and they buy up in anticipation property which is likely to provoke the action of the local authority. If they succeed in aggravating the nuisance till it is intolerable, their fortunes are made. The ratepayers at large must bear the cost of putting an end to this detestable business, and are expected at the same time to reward munificently all who have been engaged in it."

proposals. Does Mr. Chamberlain think that any attention on the part of ground landlords to the repairs and sanitation of houses would check the practices to which he is here alluding? Does he not see that it would tend rather to encourage them, by making the parties concerned more comfortable? Is vice less vicious when it is practised under perfect sanitary conditions? Or would Mr. Chamberlain turn the whole landlord class into a *police des mœurs*, and insist on their thrusting out of doors every lodger, male or female, who had not a perfectly clean bill of what is conventionally called morality? Verily we have here a *Joseph* come to judgment! And as we suppose he would hardly condemn the whole class to gallows or grape *à la* Carlyle, we may fairly ask him where they are to live during the process of repentance and amendment, if, indeed, he expects that his stringent measures will cause them to repent and amend?

Be it remembered that this process of turning people out of doors is a very unpopular one. When the owners of land or of houses resort to it for the purpose of recovering rent, it creates the utmost odium. How long would it be tolerated if the State, or a public department, or a municipality, had to bear the responsibility of such acts? And if the populace took to striking against the inspectors, and "passively resisting eviction," what force could be brought to bear that would keep order? Such things have been done when landlords and the collection of rent were concerned; is it very extravagant to surmise that they might be done if the evictions were enforced in the name of sanitation or of morality?

Differing thus widely from Mr. Chamberlain, it is somewhat satisfactory to be able to conclude with a point on which we agree with him. We refer to his criticism on Lord Salisbury's proposal to house public servants at the public expense.* Even here

---

* "What can be more unpractical than the demand that the State shall provide house-room for all its servants? Consider the difficulties raised by such a scheme. Is the accommodation to be provided free, and in addition to present salaries and wages, or is it to be charged at a fair market rate? If the

Mr. Chamberlain fails to perceive that the very same human tendencies and characteristics to which he appeals in the case of State officials would operate in the case of independent workmen; but let that pass.

Finally, be it said that to discern and state difficulties is not to create them. Any one who will think this subject out will see that a scheme which purports to cure poverty, and the moral and material evils growing out of poverty, by State regulation, is Socialism more or less diluted; and Socialism can only be made practicable by adopting a social discipline which shall be virtually undistinguishable from slavery.

---

former, then the proposition amounts to a grant of one-sixth increased remuneration over and above the ordinary rate of wages to all persons at present in the employ of the Government, and at the expense, of course, of all persons who are not officials. A sum which must be counted in millions will be added at once to the taxation of the country; but this is by no means the only objection. The grant of house accommodation must be proportioned to the size of the family—otherwise the State would become *particeps criminis* in overcrowding—and the postman with a large family of eight or ten children will receive benefits double or treble the value of what will fall to his comrades who have remained single. Again, is the accommodation offered to bear any relation to the position of the official? or is a coal-porter to have the same apartments as a confidential clerk or private secretary? If, however, the accommodation provided by the State is to be rented at a fair value to its servants, we are landed in another set of difficulties. Are all the officials to be required to avail themselves of the house-room offered them, and at the rents fixed by the Treasury? If so, there will be something like a general strike, and not half of the existing officials will surrender their independence and right to choose their own residence for their appointed share in the great Government barracks which Lord Salisbury would erect for them. If acceptance is voluntary, what is to be done with the rooms and houses which will be vacant and unoccupied by officials? Is the State to become general landlord and lodging-house keeper? *A la bonne heure!* but this is nationalisation of the land with a vengeance, and will lead us much farther than Lord Salisbury appears to imagine. Lastly, who is to insure that the evils of overcrowding and of insanitary conditions do not grow up even in the Government buildings? Are we to have a new department charged with the inspection of the private life of all the members of the Civil Service—a new *police des mœurs* created for the express benefit of Government officials?

Self-Help versus State-Help.

LIBERTY & PROPERTY DEFENCE LEAGUE.

For resisting Overlegislation, for maintaining Freedom of Contract, and for advocating Individualism as opposed to Socialism, entirely irrespective of Party Politics.

CENTRAL OFFICES:—4, WESTMINSTER CHAMBERS, VICTORIA STREET, LONDON, S.W.

COUNCIL—1883-4.

Ordinary Members:—

THE RIGHT HONOURABLE THE EARL OF WEMYSS, *Chairman.*

The Rt. Hon. Lord Bramwell.	The Rt. Hon. Lord Penzance.
Wordsworth Donisthorpe, Esq.	H. D. Pochin, Esq.
The Rt. Hon. Earl Fortescue.	H. C. Stephens, Esq.
Captain Hamber.	W. T. M'C. Torrens, Esq., M.P.
Alsager Hay Hill, Esq.	Sir Ed. W. Watkin, Bart., M.P.
J. A. Mullens, Esq.	W. Wells, Esq.
The Rt. Hon. Earl of Pembroke.	

Ex-Officio Members:—

The CHAIRMEN (or their Nominees) of Protection Societies, Companies, and Corporate Bodies formally in Correspondence with the League.

Parliamentary Committee:—

The Rt. Hon. Lord Bramwell.	The Rt. Hon. Earl of Pembroke.
Wordsworth Donisthorpe, Esq.	H. C. Stephens, Esq.

The Rt. Hon. Earl of Wemyss.

Honorary Treasurer: SIR WALTER R. FARQUHAR, BART.

Solicitors:—

Messrs. HARRIS, POWELL & SIEVEKING, 34, Essex St., Strand, W.C.

Bankers:—

Messrs. HERRIES, FARQUHAR & CO., 16, St. James's Street, S.W.

Auditors:—

Messrs. GREY, PRIDEAUX & BOOKER, 48, Lincoln's Inn Fields, W.C.

Secretary: W. C. CROFTS.

PROVINCIAL BRANCHES:—

ENGLAND—LIVERPOOL: *Hon. Secretary*, FRANCIS HARTLEY, ESQ., Castle Chambers, 26, Castle Street.

MANCHESTER: [*appointment pending.*]

LEEDS: *Hon. Secretary*, WALTER ROWLEY, ESQ., 74, Albion Street.

SHEFFIELD: *Hon. Secretary*, PERCY SORBY, ESQ., 11, George Street.

NOTTINGHAM: [*appointment pending.*]

YORK: *Hon. Secretary*, F. H. ANDERSON, ESQ., 41, Stonegate.

BRISTOL: *Hon. Secretary*, H. J. BROWN, ESQ., 43, High Street.

PLYMOUTH: *Hon. Secretary*, R. S. CLARKE, ESQ., 4 Athenæum Terrace.

BOURNEMOUTH: *Hon. Secretary*, J. R. PRETYMAN, ESQ., Richmond Lodge.

SCOTLAND—GLASGOW: *Hon. Secretary*, C. J. MACLEAN, ESQ., 81, Bath Street.

ABERDEENSHIRE: *Hon. Secretary*, Colonel W. ROSS-KING, Tertowie House, Kinaldie.

THE League opposes all attempts to introduce the State as competitor or regulator into the various departments of social activity and industry, which would otherwise be spontaneously and adequately conducted by private enterprise.

Questions of the structure or constitution of the State and those of foreign policy do not come within the scope of the League. It is exclusively concerned with the internal functions or duties of the State.

During the last 15 years all interests in the country have successively suffered at the hands of the State an increasing loss of their self-government. These apparently disconnected invasions of individual freedom of action by the central authority are in reality so many instances of a general movement towards State-Socialism, the deadening effect of which on all branches of industry and originality the working classes will be the first to feel.

Each interest conducting its self-defence without any reference to the others has, on every occasion, hitherto failed to oppose successfully the full force of this movement concentrated in turn against itself by the permanent officials and the government in power for the time being.

The League resists every particular case of this common evil by securing the co-operation of all persons individually opposed to the principle of State-Socialism in all or *any one* of its instances, and by focussing into a system of mutual defence the forces of the "Defence Associations" and "Protection Societies" of the various interests of the country.

As regards such protection societies, companies, and corporate bodies, this co-operation is effected without any interference with the independent action of each body on matters specially affecting its own interest.

Each society passes a resolution formally placing itself in correspondence with the League. The League in return supplies every such society with information concerning each fresh symptom of State interference; it places the various societies and interests in communication with one another with a view to their mutual assistance inside and outside parliament; and, at the same time, it combines for the common end the forces of the several societies and interests with those of the League itself and its members in both Houses of Parliament.

The chairman (or his nominee) of every society, company or corporate body thus in correspondence with the League is an *ex-officio* member of the Council of the League, and receives notice to attend all its meetings. The corporate action of the League in every case of overlegislation where any interest is affected is regulated by the decision of the ordinary members of Council, acting in conjunction with its *ex-officio* members.

Persons wishing to join the League are requested to send their subscription (voluntary from five shillings upwards) and address to Messrs. Herries, Farquhar & Co., Bankers, 16, St. James's Street, S.W. Particulars and Publications of the League, can be had from the Secretary, W. C. Crofts, at the Central Offices.

Printed by G. Harmsworth & Co.,
Tavistock Street, Covent Garden, London, W.C.

Printed by Libri Plureos GmbH in Hamburg,
Germany